GETTING THE GOLD

A Play In Three Acts

By
P. J. BARRY

July 1989

strong supporter.
Best,
PJ.

SAMUEL FRENCH, INC.
45 West 25th Street NEW YORK 10010
7623 Sunset Boulevard HOLLYWOOD 90046
LONDON TORONTO

ISBN 0 573 69092 8 Printed in U.S.A.

IMPORTANT BILLING AND CREDIT REQUIREMENTS

All producers of GETTING THE GOLD *must* give credit to the Author of the Play in all programs distributed in connection with performances of the Play and in all instances in which the title of the Play appears for purposes of advertising, publicizing or otherwise exploiting the Play and/or a production. The name of the Author *must* also appear on a separate line, in which no other name appears, immediately following the title, and *must* appear in size of type not less than fifty percent the size of the title type.

To my sons, Matthew and Neill
and my daughter, Nina

Long Island's Only Professional Resident Theatre Company

CLINTON J. ATKINSON
Artistic Director

RALPH J. STALTER, JR.
Managing Director

GETTING THE GOLD

A World Premiere
by
P.J. Barry
with

Don Billett · Nancy-Elizabeth Kammer · Marilyn Rockafellow
Amy Ryan · Anne Shropshire

Scenery By	*Costumes By*	*Lighting By*
DANIEL CONWAY	CLAUDIA STEPHENS	JOHN HICKEY

Stage Manager — DAVID WAHL

Directed by
CLINTON J. ATKINSON

May 31 - June 19, 1988

Long Island Stage operates under an agreement between the League of Resident Theatres (LORT) and Actors' Equity Association, the Union of Professional Actors and Stage Managers in the United States.

The Director and Artistic Director is a member of the Society of Stage Directors and Choreographers, an independent, national labor union.

Long Island Stage is a not-for-profit organization, supported with public funds from the New York State Council on the Arts, the Natural Heritage Trust, and the Nassau County Office of Cultural Development. Contributions are also received from individuals, businesses, and private foundations.

GETTING THE GOLD premiered at Long Island Stage, Clinton J. Atkinson and Ralph J. Stalter, Jr., respectively Artistic and Managing Directors, under the direction of Mr. Atkinson, with scenery by Daniel Conway, costumes by Claudia Stephens, lighting by John Hickey, and stage management by David Wahl, with the following cast:

HARRIET CAMPBELL . . . . Nancy-Elizabeth Kammer

PEG CAMPBELL . . . . Marilyn Rockafellow

JILL CAMPBELL . . . . Amy Ryan

BRAD CAMPBELL . . . . Don Billett

CAMMY . . . . Anne Shropshire

THE CHARACTERS

CAMMY — A spry, charming strong-willed woman of 80, no longer as physically active as she'd like to be. She looks younger.

PEG CAMPBELL — Cammy's daughter, 50. A striking trim woman.

BRAD — Peg's husband. A tall, athletic 55, still in good shape.

HARRIET — Their oldest daughter, 25. Pretty and plump.

JILL — Their youngest daughter, 20. Beautiful and slim.

THE SETTING

A comfortable sun room in the home of Brad and Peg Campbell near Westerly, Rhode Island.

At left upstage there is an entrance into a hallway where a stairway is partially visible. This hallway leads to other parts of the two-story rambling house, and off left into the dining room and kitchen area. At right downstage there are glass paneled doors onto the patio (beyond a two-acre backyard, flower garden, tool shed and swimming pool). Far up right is a small vestibule area and entrance into Cammy's room (Also, unseen, is a patio entrance into Cammy's room).

The room has a sofa, coffee table, stuffed chairs, end tables, lamps, a small secretary, bookshelves and, most important, a card table with a jigsaw puzzle.

THE TIME

A few years ago. Early June.

ACT I
Scene 1 A Friday. About 6:30 P.M.
Scene 2 About 1 A. M.

ACT II
Scene 1 Saturday. Early morning.
Scene 2 About noon.

ACT III
Scene 1 Later. Mid-afternoon
Scene 2 That evening.

NOTES

The play can also be performed in two acts by dividing each act into three scenes.

The use of a cane by Cammy is optional.

GETTING THE GOLD

ACT I
Scene 1

SCENE: A comfortable sun room in the home of BRAD and PEG Campbell near Westerly, Rhode Island. A Friday evening, about 6:30 P.M. It is early June.

AT RISE: HARRIET sits alone. She has a drink.

PEG Enters.

HARRIET. Where is the birthday girl?

PEG. Changing for dinner.

HARRIET. Is she still dressing herself?

PEG. What kind of a question is that?

HARRIET. A silly one. Cammy will be dressing herself for her funeral.

PEG. Will you be nice?

HARRIET. What does Doctor Potter say?

PEG. *(retrieving her drink)* She appears to be in excellent health ... except for the arthritis in her left hand and a little deafness which she refuses to admit to. But this past week she's beginning to worry me. *(pause)* She's making up stories again.

HARRIET. Back to the Titanic, huh? Glug, glug, glug.

PEG. Stop it. Earlier this week she went on about a woodpecker pecking on her windows.

HARRIET. Tap, tap, tap.

PEG. From one window to the other.

HARRIET. Knock, knock, knock.

PEG. Stop.

HARRIET. It may be a new species. A windowpecker.

PEG. I think this could be serious. And I want you to be nice to her. It's her eightieth birthday.

HARRIET. I'm here. I came for the celebration. If she behaves, I'll behave.

PEG. Please.

HARRIET. Can I borrow three thousand dollars? *(no response)* Can I?

PEG. *(pause)* Since we moved here we seldom see you. One Thanksgiving, one Christmas. Twice in two years.

HARRIET. This makes three in three years.

PEG. And when you do come you ask for money.

HARRIET. I wouldn't ask if I didn't need it. I have to get a new apartment.

PEG. What's wrong with the one you've got?

HARRIET. It's Michael's. I let mine go when I moved in with him.

PEG. A little foolish, Harriet.

HARRIET. A lot foolish, Mother.

PEG. I thought you two were getting along.

HARRIET. Not anymore.

PEG. In the future use a little common sense.

HARRIET. Thanks for your concern. Will you let me

borrow the money?

PEG. You've borrowed enough as it is ... which you have *not* paid back. No. Neither you nor Jill have any concept of money. You were both spoiled. Furthermore, your father and I—

(JILL Enters, carrying a plant.)

JILL. Another African violet for Cammy.

PEG. From whom?

JILL. The Bentleys in Hartford.

PEG. Oh, how thoughtful of them.

JILL. Look. It's droopy, pooped out. This leaf looks chewed up.

PEG. It does. How did you get this? Was it delivered? I didn't hear the bell.

JILL. I was down by the gate. Fenwick Florists, Rhode Island's finest, drove up—

HARRIET. Cammy won't approve.

PEG. I don't approve. They wouldn't do this unless it was from out of town. Do they think we won't make a fuss? I'm surprised at Fenwicks.

HARRIET. Oh, so am I. Tsk, tsk, tsk...

(BRAD Enters. Wears a shirt, tie, jacket; carries a drink.)

BRAD. What about Fenwicks?

PEG. They just brought this for Cammy ... from the Bentleys in Hartford.

BRAD. George and Myra.

HARRIET. Good old George and Myra.

BRAD. Nice of them to remember Cammy.

PEG. Look at the plant, Brad.

JILL. The more you look at it the more it droops.

PEG. And this leaf looks chewed up.

HARRIET. And pooped out.

BRAD. Why would Fenwicks send a drooping thing like that?

HARRIET. Cammy will soon have the investigation underway. *(Mimics CAMMY.)* "It's disgraceful."

PEG. It is disgraceful. George and Myra paid good money for this.

HARRIET. Good old George and Myra.

BRAD. Jill, do you want anything to drink?

JILL. I'll get it, Dad.

BRAD. Do you want a refill, Harriet?

HARRIET. No thanks.

PEG. I wish Cammy would hurry. Dinner's almost ready.

BRAD. Peg, we'll give her time to sip her martini out here in her favorite spot. Tonight, let's accommodate her. You get to be eighty only once. *(Exits.)*

HARRIET. Wise man.

JILL. *(PEG starts out after BRAD.)* Need any help, Mom?

PEG. Just the water glasses, if you don't mind. *(Exits.)*

JILL. Be there in a minute!

HARRIET. The crystal goblets.

JILL. No doubt.

HARRIET. Nothing but the best for Cammy's birthday dinner. *(They both laugh.)*

JILL. I'm surprised you showed at all.

HARRIET. I'm a masochist. Ask dear mother.

JILL. You told her about Michael.

HARRIET. Yes.

JILL. What did she say?

HARRIET. That I was a foolish bitch for moving in with him in the first place.

JILL. She said that? — She did not. Foolish maybe, but not bitch.

HARRIET. Actually, I came home to get a loan from her or Dad. She said no.

JILL. She would. They're having problems.

HARRIET. Who's he chasing around here?

JILL. He's not chasing anybody.

HARRIET. Ha!!

JILL. They're having *financial* problems.

HARRIET. With Cammy on call?

JILL. Dad didn't get a Christmas bonus and then no raise. When I came home for Easter, he suggested that I get a job for the summer to help with expenses at school.

HARRIET. I thought you were going to Europe this summer with friends?

JILL. I'll be waiting table on the Cape.

HARRIET. *(Laughs.)* You won't last a week.

JILL. I can do it.

HARRIET. Well, they may be having a financial squeeze right now, but if they're in real trouble Mother dear can always get it from Cammy. So don't worry about flunking waitressing. Of course, all our problems would be solved tonight if Cammy blew out her candles and fell over dead in her birthday cake.

JILL. Harriet.

HARRIET. Mother dear would inherit about ... six million dollars. She'd be grief stricken, but generous. You could go to Europe this summer ... have your tuition guaranteed ... I'd get my loan. But Cammy won't drop dead in her birthday cake.

JILL. You really are demented.

HARRIET. How about *this.* I sneak into Cammy's room, smother her with a pillow ... then push Mother into the pool, jump to the rescue but drown her instead ... and then *we'd* inherit all of Cammy's gold. I know what you're thinking, Mother will leave everything to Father. Well—

JILL. Why don't you spare your family. Just go back to New York, push Michael into a cake or drown him or—

HARRIET. I tried. But he got the knife away from me.

JILL. He *what?*

HARRIET. I had to work one weekend but finished early, came home and found him in bed with another woman. Of course I made a scene. He called me a fat cow and told me he didn't want me anymore. I saw red and went for him with a carving knife.

JILL. My God!

HARRIET. Well, he slapped me, took the knife away and told me to clear out of *his* apartment — *Don't* say I provoked him.

JILL. What are you going to do?

HARRIET. *That's* why I'm here, dummy. New apartments cost money.

(CAMMY Enters by the patio door.)

JILL. Oh, Cammy, how pretty you look. You look ... I can't think of the word.

CAMMY. Radiant?

JILL. Uh huh. Radiant.

CAMMY. I like that. Radiant. Thank you.

JILL. You're welcome.

CAMMY. You think this color is becoming?

JILL. Uh huh.

CAMMY. It's not too youthful?

JILL. No.

CAMMY. Harriet?

HARRIET. No. You look ... radiant.

CAMMY. Thank you.

HARRIET. You're welcome.

CAMMY. What's that? *Another* African violet?

JILL. Uh huh.

CAMMY. Oh. How nice. That makes seven. Who sent it?

JILL. The Bentleys.

CAMMY. Charles and Sarah.

HARRIET. George and Myra. Charles and Sarah were the Colemans.

CAMMY. Yes, you're right, Harriet. The Bentleys. George and Myra, yes.

HARRIET. *(muttering)* Good old George and Myra.

CAMMY. *(overlapping)* How sweet of them. I wonder what ever happened to the Colemans? I haven't heard from Charles and Sarah in years.

HARRIET. They're dead.

CAMMY. Both of them?

JILL. Yes.

HARRIET. That's why you haven't heard from them in years.

CAMMY. Oh, how awful. One does lose track. *(now examining the new African violet)* Oh, how awful! Look at this. Look, Jill. Look, Harriet. It's all...

HARRIET. Pooped out.

CAMMY. Disgraceful! George and Myra were cheated.

HARRIET. Poor old George and Myra.

CAMMY. Well, something must be done about it. *(Checks her watch.)* It's twenty of seven. When did they deliver this?

JILL. Ten minutes ago.

CAMMY. They must still be open.

HARRIET. Wait until morning.

CAMMY. Why should I? I'll call them now. *(Starts toward the door to her room.)*

HARRIET. I can drive you there in the morning. Your outrage will be much more effective in person.

CAMMY. Let's plan on that. Tomorrow is Saturday. On Saturdays we have breakfast at nine thirty. We can leave at ten-ten.

HARRIET. Ten-ten sounds good.

CAMMY. Splendid. I'm so surprised at Fenwick's. Jill, would you ask your father to please bring me my martini now?

JILL. Sure.

CAMMY. Don't say "Sure." Say, "Yes," or "Of course"

or even "Surely" ... but not "Sure." It sounds so common.

JILL. Sure. *(starting off again)*

CAMMY. *Of course.* And don't slouch, dear. Stand up straight like your mother.

JILL. I'm not slouching. It's just the fatigue after my finals. Don't judge me, just try and understand me. *(Waves and Exits.)*

CAMMY. *(pause)* You both play games with me. *(pause)* You disapprove of me.

HARRIET. We don't disapprove of you, Cammy. We simply never agree with you.

CAMMY. Jill is a little thin, don't you think?

HARRIET. There is no such thing as "a little thin."

CAMMY. Well, you were born chubby. And that sweet tooth of yours. You never did curb it.

HARRIET. Thank you. I need to be reminded.

CAMMY. You can conquer the problem. Stick to a diet, dear. Exercise.

HARRIET. *(rising)* I promised that I would be nice to you on your birthday.

CAMMY. Well, I should hope so.

HARRIET. You're not making it easy. *(Starts away.)*

CAMMY. Harriet. Wait. One minute ... while we're alone. *(Lowers her voice.)* I've got to tell *someone. Someone* is trying to kill me.

HARRIET. *(pause)* You've lived eighty years. Take it as it comes. *(Starts off again.)*

CAMMY. I am not joking — Harriet, please. I *need* to discuss it with you. *(HARRIET hesitates.)* If anyone comes into the room, I will change the subject.

HARRIET. *(pause)* Who's the suspect?

CAMMY. Your father...

HARRIET. Ah. And Mother, too?

CAMMY. You mean conspirators? Well, I hadn't thought...

HARRIET. *(overlapping)* What do you want me to do? Confront them? Come on, Cammy, why should they want to kill you?

CAMMY. Just listen.

HARRIET. I'm listening.

CAMMY. Last week I found a banana peel just outside my patio door. Now. How did a banana peel get there? It was placed there so I would have an accident. So I would fall and seriously injure myself, break my neck. Don't look at me with the smirky expression—

HARRIET. Anybody throw a custard pie?

CAMMY. No joking and no smirking, please. Also there was the black cat. Two days ago I walked into my bathroom and there in my bathtub was a black cat, dead. Your father said that my screen door onto the patio must've been open — but it wasn't — he said it was obviously a stray that had wandered in and chosen to drop dead in my bathtub. But I think it was placed there to frighten me to death. After all, I *have* had one serious stroke and—

HARRIET. What about the woodpecker?

CAMMY. I said a black cat.

HARRIET. But what about the woodpecker?

CAMMY. What woodpecker?

HARRIET. *(pause)* Do you want anything from the kitchen?

CAMMY. I want you to listen.

HARRIET. I did, my dear, I did. *(Exits.)*

CAMMY. *(pause)* Oh. Oh, the woodpecker ... oh, yes.

(JILL returns, carrying a martini and a glass of wine for herself.)

JILL. *(lightly)* Here's your poison. *(CAMMY looks startled.)* No, no, I'm joking. *(Laughs.)* Not on your birthday. *(Laughs again, wanders to table, sipping her glass of wine. On the table a jigsaw puzzle is in progress.)* Whose face? And don't make me guess.

CAMMY. Samuel Clemens.

JILL. Oh.

CAMMY. Mark Twain. I met him once.

JILL. I know.

CAMMY. I wasn't even knee high.

JILL. Just a slip of a girl.

CAMMY. Yes. *(JILL sits at puzzle table, works on puzzle.)* Jill, I want to discuss something with you.

JILL. Please don't say anything about my hair. It's just highlighted. And I don't care if you don't like it, I like it.

(PEG returns.)

PEG. Don't talk to your grandmother in that tone of voice.

JILL. What tone of voice?

PEG. Disrespectfully.

JILL. I was being direct, not disrespectful. I'm trying to

become more ... assertive...

PEG. Oh, you found the end of his moustache. Good.

JILL. I feel so dependent when I come home.

PEG. *(affectionately rumpling JILL'S hair)* Oh, stop.

CAMMY. *(Sits.)* Is that why you're going to waitress this summer? To prove your independence?

PEG. It's admirable.

CAMMY. Who said it wasn't?

JILL. I want to see if I'm capable of sticking it out.

PEG. You will.

JILL. You did.

PEG. I never waited tables. Tough job.

JILL. You became a nurse. That took guts. You showed your—

CAMMY. *(overlapping)* You don't want to be a nurse.

JILL. No.

CAMMY. Thank God.

JILL. You didn't approve of Mom becoming a nurse?

CAMMY. I certainly did not. She defied me. And her father.

JILL. How brave.

PEG. Maybe. But it was very unpleasant.

(BRAD returns.)

BRAD. How's your drink, Cammy?

(TELEPHONE rings offstage.)

CAMMY. There's a slightly tart taste. Could it be—

(HARRIET is seen in the hallway, then moving off.)

HARRIET. I've got it!

(TELEPHONE rings again.)

BRAD. I'm trying a new vermouth.

PEG. Oh, you're wearing your new dress.

CAMMY. I never thought you'd notice.

JILL. Doesn't she look terrific!

CAMMY. Earlier, you said "radiant." I prefer that.

PEG and BRAD. You look radiant. *(They all laugh.)*

(HARRIET returns eating a handful of wheat thins.)

HARRIET. It's for you, Dad.

BRAD. Who is it?

HARRIET. An old pal. Calling from New York. Kay Tobin.

BRAD. Thank you, Harriet. *(Exits.)*

HARRIET. *(pause)* I wonder what she wants.

CAMMY. Who is Kay Tobin?

HARRIET. An old pal. *(Sits.)*

PEG. *(to JILL:)* What about setting the water glasses, you.

JILL. Whoops. Sorry. Practically done. *(and dashes off)*

CAMMY. Peg, who is Kay Tobin?

PEG. *(retrieving her drink)* I believe she used to be one of Brad's assistants when the company was in New York.

HARRIET. His only assistant. When the company

relocated here, she didn't come along. Did she, Mom?

PEG. No. They were cutting costs.

HARRIET. What could she want after all this time?

PEG. You can ask your father when he gets off the phone.

CAMMY. Oh. She was that woman.

HARRIET. Cammy tells me someone is trying to kill her.

PEG. *(startled, to CAMMY:)* Did you say that?

CAMMY. No. I said—

HARRIET. She found a banana peel outside her patio door. Someone wanted her to slip and fall and break her neck, she said.

PEG. You never told me about any banana peel.

HARRIET. Why would she? It's you or Dad ready to do her in.

CAMMY. You must have misunderstood me.

PEG. She's watching too much television, and reading too many mysteries.

HARRIET. Will she be sent to her room without any birthday dinner for telling lies?

CAMMY. You're confused, child.

HARRIET. Well, what about the dead black cat?

PEG. That isn't a lie. It scared all of us. How it got into the house we'll never know. *(pause)* Let's go into dinner.

HARRIET. Mother. When Cammy finishes her drink.

CAMMY. You'll just have to wait a little.

PEG. *(testily)* No, I don't have to. Dinner is ready.

(JILL returns.)

HARRIET. Mother. It's Cammy's eightieth birthday. Please be nice.

PEG. *(to CAMMY:)* You can be an exasperating woman! *(Exits.)*

JILL. *(pause)* What happened?

CAMMY. Thank you, Harriet.

HARRIET. *(Rises.)* Forgive me. But it's best to get that kind of thing out in the open ... before someone gets hurt. *(Exits.)*

JILL. Mom was angry. What did I miss? *(Retrieves her glass of wine.)*

CAMMY. It was supposed to be a secret; but Harriet didn't believe me. So she told your mother.

JILL. Told her what?

CAMMY. About the banana peel. And the black cat.

JILL. What are you talking about?

CAMMY. Someone's trying to kill me.

JILL. Huh?

CAMMY. Your father ... or ... or perhaps ... even your mother...

JILL. *(Laughs.)* Oh, Cammy...

CAMMY. I don't want to believe it either ... but I'm afraid I must.

JILL. Do you still have Grampa's pistol?

CAMMY. What? Oh, yes. Yes, I do. Somewhere. Why?

JILL. To protect yourself. Get them before they get you. Pow! *(Exits.)*

(Lights quickly fade.)

Scene 2

SCENE: The same. Around 1 A.M.

AT RISE: HARRIET is sitting in the dark, MOONLIGHT brightens her area. She wears a light robe over pajamas. She is eating cake and ice cream.

A LIGHT is turned on upstairs, lighting the stairs. BRAD comes down the stairs. He is wearing a robe and is barefooted. He crosses the hallway and Exits, another LIGHT goes on, a moment, it goes off and he comes into the hallway, now carrying two small brandy glasses. He turns on the LIGHTS for the sun room and Enters, and picks up a bottle of brandy. Turning, he is surprised to see HARRIET.

BRAD. *(pause)* Couldn't sleep?

HARRIET. No.

BRAD. It's after one.

HARRIET. My watch is working.

BRAD. What's that?

HARRIET. Birthday cake. And ice cream. Vanilla fudge.

BRAD. Didn't you have enough?

HARRIET. I guess not. *(pause)* Having *more* brandy?

BRAD. Do you want some?

HARRIET. With this? No, thank you. *Two* glasses?

BRAD. Your mother.

HARRIET. Oh, how romantic.

BRAD. We still have our moments.

HARRIET. She's such an understanding lady.

BRAD. Having problems with the boyfriend?

HARRIET. Yes. He wants me out. Mother told you.

BRAD. She mentioned it.

HARRIET. And the subject was quickly dismissed.

BRAD. You've been through this kind of thing before.

HARRIET. I have to get a new apartment. I need money, Dad.

BRAD. Your mother told you—

HARRIET. I'm asking you.

BRAD. You'll have to handle it yourself this time. Sell your car. A car isn't a necessity in New York.

HARRIET. I'm not asking for a lot. Three thousand would do it. I only owe you...

BRAD. You owe us six thousand. *(Pours himself some brandy.)*

HARRIET. *(pause)* Do you want me to beg?

BRAD. Your mother and I do not have any money to spare.

HARRIET. Maybe I should try Cammy?

BRAD. Try.

HARRIET. She's acting a little out of it.

BRAD. Sort of.

HARRIET. She told me that someone is trying to kill her.

BRAD. Did she?

HARRIET. You or mother.

BRAD. And once again she survived the Titanic ... "just a slip of a girl."

HARRIET. *(chiming in)* "... just a slip of a girl." Is she getting senile?

BRAD. It's to be expected at her age.

HARRIET. What about two thousand? I could squeeze by with that.

BRAD. *(overlapping)* You make a good salary. What do you do with it?

HARRIET. I made a mistake with Michael. I'm admitting it. I'm asking for help.

BRAD. Two weeks ago all company executives had to take salary cuts.

HARRIET. Tragic.

BRAD. Yes, it is.

HARRIET. I'm sure two thousand wouldn't—

BRAD. No, Harriet. Nothing. Take care of yourself. You're a big girl now. *(Starts off.)*

HARRIET. *(angered)* Why do you treat me like this? I ask for help, and you and mother turn your backs!

BRAD. You always did throw a tantrum when you didn't get what you wanted.

HARRIET. You prick.

BRAD. Don't talk to me like that.

HARRIET. "Don't talk to me like that." — You're a prick, a bastard, a stingy, womanizing sonofabitch!

BRAD. *(overlapping)* Shut up, Harriet.

HARRIET. Mother should've divorced you.

BRAD. Ancient history.

HARRIET. Oh, no. Three years to be exact ... before you moved here. I remember it well.

BRAD. Couldn't wait to tell your mother, couldn't wait to cause her pain.

HARRIET. I caused no pain. You were the one getting it on with your ravishing assistant. I just told her I caught the bad boy with his pants down; she deserved to be told. Why *did* Kay Tobin call you tonight?

BRAD. I told you at dinner. *(carrying the glasses and bottle starts off again)*

HARRIET. Now that we're alone, confide in me, *Dad*. Why did she *really* call you tonight?

BRAD. *(overlapping, hesitating, more emphatically) I told you at dinner.*

HARRIET. *(overlapping)* I met her at a cocktail party recently. I said to her: "Are you still servicing my father?" And she said: "Not often enough."

BRAD. Cute story.

HARRIET. How do you manage it? Do you drive to Providence or Boston? New London? New London's good and sleazy.

(CAMMY Enters from outside patio door. Overlapping.)

CAMMY. I saw the light ...

BRAD. You've been awake?

CAMMY. Oh, yes. I was sitting up in the dark ... looking out at the night. The full moon. Beautiful. Someone's swimming in the pool.

BRAD. Did you take a close look?

CAMMY. I don't walk around the grounds in the dark. I could fall.

BRAD. It could be a prowler. *(Sets down glasses and bottle.)*

HARRIET. Prowlers swim in pools in the middle of the night.

BRAD. Probably Jill.

HARRIET. Uh huh.

BRAD. I'll check. *(Exits.)*

CAMMY. Yes. It's probably Jill.

HARRIET. Probably.

CAMMY. Did you tell him what I told you? Of course you did. You told your mother ... why wouldn't you tell your father? You should not have told either of them. You have exposed me in a most dangerous way.

HARRIET. If I believed that my life was in danger I wouldn't sit around talking about it, I would do something about it.

CAMMY. *(sitting at the puzzle table)* I'm not sure what to do. I have no proof.

HARRIET. Hire a bodyguard. You can afford it. You can afford ten of them ... if you think there's a need.

CAMMY. A bodyguard?

HARRIET. Like the President.

CAMMY. What President?

HARRIET. Of the United States.

CAMMY. Oh, him. No, I don't think so. Bodyguard. You wind up with no privacy.

HARRIET. Without one, you could wind up dead.

CAMMY. Oh, it's certainly a valid suggestion. However—

HARRIET. Can I borrow three thousand dollars from you?

CAMMY. Three thousand dollars?

HARRIET. Yes.

CAMMY. No. I'm not as foolish as your parents.

HARRIET. Please.

CAMMY. Why do you need it?

HARRIET. A new apartment. I have to move. I've been living with Michael in *his* apartment

CAMMY. Where do you find these young men?

HARRIET. Be a sport, Cammy.

CAMMY. I'll do no such thing. However, I will offer you some sound advice. Try celibacy for awhile ... until you have sorted out your emotions. Don't be so eager to jump into another one-sided arrangement. You're not planning to do that, are you?

HARRIET. Well, I am a bit intrigued by a new man in the office. He's a black, bald, Catholic midget.

CAMMY. *(pause)* You're playing games.

HARRIET. *(rising, getting into her slippers)* How's the Titanic?

CAMMY. What?

HARRIET. Didn't you survive the Titanic? Mother and Dad said—

CAMMY. *(snappishly)* I was never on the Titanic. It was my second cousin. Ruth. She was just a slip of a girl. Ruth. Not me.

HARRIET. Are you sure?

BRAD. *(returning from the patio)* It's Jill.

CAMMY. Oh. Good.

HARRIET. I'm going back to bed. Goodnight.

CAMMY. You will drive me to Fenwick Florists in the morning ... as you promised.

HARRIET. We'll see.

CAMMY. *(to BRAD:)* I'm going to exchange that disgraceful African violet — The bowl, Harriet.

HARRIET. Oh. Sorry. *(Returns, picks up the bowl.)* I'm such a bad little girl.

BRAD. Goodnight, Harriet.

HARRIET. 'Night, *Daddy.* *(Hesitates.)* Sweet dreams everybody. *(Exits.)*

CAMMY. *(pause)* Harriet didn't come for my birthday. She came to get money. She's angry. I said no.

BRAD. She wanted money from me, too. I said the same.

CAMMY. She'll get the money from Peg.

BRAD. Not this time. We don't have it.

CAMMY. Are you having financial difficulties?

BRAD. Times are not good.

CAMMY. You haven't discussed it with me.

BRAD. Have we ever?

CAMMY. I've contributed my share since I've come here to live with you.

BRAD. A very generous one.

CAMMY. Yes. Yes, it is.

BRAD. You could make it a larger share, say a million dollars.

CAMMY. *(Laughs.)* Harriet only wanted to borrow three thousand.

BRAD. I said nothing about borrowing, Cammy. I'm talking about a contribution ... to your daughter and your son-in-law ... in troubled times.

CAMMY. *(pause)* And if I don't?

BRAD. *(Laughs.)* I'm not serious.

CAMMY. *(long pause)* How do you intend to end my life?

BRAD. We haven't decided. Do you have a preference?

CAMMY. You said *we.* It is both of you.

BRAD. If you're convinced that someone is trying to kill you, then call the police.

CAMMY. I would. But I need ... I need...

BRAD. Evidence? Do you want me to call them for you? *(crossing the room toward the hallway)* I play golf with Inspector Connors. I can call him.

CAMMY. No.

BRAD. Are you sure, Cammy?

CAMMY. Look at the time ... I ... I have to think this through.

BRAD. Can I book you passage on the Titanic?

CAMMY. What?

BRAD. How's the woodpecker doing?

CAMMY. What?

BRAD. Any black cats hanging around?

CAMMY. You are—

BRAD. *(overlapping)* Seen any more banana peels? — Would you like some brandy?

CAMMY. What? *(HARRIET Enters from up left, goes upstairs.)*

(JILL Enters, drying her hair, wears a bikini.)

JILL. Oh, it was heaven! The water is just right. *(BRAD pours himself more brandy.)* Why's everybody up? Never mind. Nobody could sleep with a full moon like this. Oh, I feel so good. Now I'll sleep like a baby. 'Night, Dad. *(Kisses him.)*

BRAD. 'Night, hon.

(PEG comes down the stairs, hesitates by the doorway.)

JILL. *(kissing CAMMY)* 'Night, Cammy.

CAMMY. Goodnight, dear.

PEG. Get out of that wet bathing suit. You'll catch cold.

JILL. *(lightly)* I hadn't planned on sleeping in it ... but thank you for reminding me.

PEG. *(lightly)* You're welcome.

JILL. 'Night. *(Kisses her mother and starts off upstairs.)* 'Night, everybody. *(and is gone, a chorus of "goodnight")*

PEG. What happened to my brandy?

BRAD. Sorry. *(Gives her a quick kiss.)* It was busy down here.

PEG. I met Harriet upstairs. She looked ... grim.

BRAD. She tried to borrow money from you, from me and from Cammy. No success.

PEG. It's time she learned to handle her finances. *(to CAMMY: in reference to the puzzle)* Oh, you found his left eye. He has such dark eyes.

CAMMY. It's shadow.

PEG. Yes. I think you're right. Couldn't you sleep?

CAMMY. *(to BRAD:)* Why did you say that to me? About booking passage on the Titanic.

BRAD. I *asked* you if you wanted me to call the police.

CAMMY. Then you asked about booking passage for me on the Titanic.

BRAD. No. I asked you if you'd like some brandy. Besides, the Titanic sailed and sank ... long ago.

CAMMY. I know that, Jeffrey. Why is everyone talking

about it tonight and *saying* I sailed on it? That time ... after my stroke ... it was to be expected ... I was ... disoriented. I remember thinking it was me and not my cousin Ruth who survived that disaster. Is Ruth still living in California?

PEG. Yes...

BRAD. *(sitting on couch)* I'm Brad, not Jeffrey.

CAMMY. Did I call you Jeffrey?

BRAD. Yes.

PEG. What is this talk about the police?

BRAD. Your mother seems to think her life is in danger.

CAMMY. *(to PEG:)* Did I just call him Jeffrey?

PEG. Yes, you did.

CAMMY. I see. Well ... the hour is late. And I'm now an octogenarian. Therefore, I am entitled to ... crisscross thoughts and names.

PEG. You should be in bed.

CAMMY. *Should I?* My days are numbered, you know that. I shall attempt to remain alert and to—

PEG. Mother, you're just wearing yourself out. I want you to stop this.

CAMMY. You made plans *together.* I feel that now.

PEG. I don't want to hear anymore ... is that clear? You need your sleep. Now please go to your room.

CAMMY. Go to my room.

PEG. Yes.

CAMMY. Like a child.

PEG. You're behaving like one.

CAMMY. Your father would never permit—

PEG. *(annoyed)* My father has been dead for years — It's

nice to imagine what it would — Oh, how do you get me into these stupid arguments? Go to your room and be still.

CAMMY. *(rising, growing more indignant)* I am an adult!

PEG. *(more annoyed)* You shouldn't be up at this time of night. Go-to-your-room. You're turning into a silly old woman.

CAMMY. You will not succeed. *(Exits into her room.)*

PEG. *(Crosses the room ready to slam the door after her.)* She gets something in that mind of hers and she won't let go! *(Pause, closes the door.)* Oh, she can get me crazy! She's growing more and more impossible. I should never have brought her here.

BRAD. You didn't have much choice.

PEG. *(Sits at puzzle table.)* I could've left her in New York.

BRAD. You thought she would die.

PEG. She's acting in that same peculiar way ... just before she had her stroke ... even more irrationally. And you ... that talk about the Titanic and police ... you *know* she's easily upset these days. *(Rises.)*

BRAD. I know. What are we going to do about her?

PEG. I'd like to give her a good swift kick if I thought it would do any good. Oh, I'm so worried about her and this is no way to react.

BRAD. She accused you, she accused me of trying to murder her.

PEG. I don't want her in one of those places. *(calming down)* Oh, I know they have special ones ... the best that money can buy. She's not really irrational, just—

BRAD. — a *little* irrational. Soon she'll have the police here.

PEG. Are you worried about the police? Do you think she'll really call them? Oh, let her. It's all so ridiculous. She's just getting older. But it hurts her ... it hurts me. We just have to live with it. She's my mother! Oh, God ... I don't want to talk about her anymore. Let's go back to bed. *(Picks up her glass and bottle.)*

BRAD. And make love again.

PEG. *(pause)* You're greedy tonight.

BRAD. I'm always greedy. *(Holds out his glass.)*

PEG. When I met Harriet upstairs do you know what she said? *(Sets her glass down.)*

BRAD. She said we never loved her.

PEG. *(pouring him some brandy)* She said: "Is Dad running off again with Kay Tobin?"

BRAD. If you're unhappy ... make someone else feel worse.

PEG. *(Sets down bottle, sits on couch.)* Why would she say that?

BRAD. I just told you why.

PEG. Was that all Kay Tobin wanted?

BRAD. Yes.

PEG. A letter of recommendation?

BRAD. That's why she called.

PEG. She's moving to San Francisco?

BRAD. That's what she said.

PEG. Did she want you to go with her?

BRAD. Can I help it if she's still madly in love with me?

PEG. That's not funny.

BRAD. It's not meant to be.

PEG. Is she still "madly" in love with you?

BRAD. Does it matter?

PEG. *(pause)* We all are.

BRAD. Still madly in love with me?

PEG. Yes.

BRAD. You? *(Draws her to him.)*

PEG. You still excite me so much. The nicest part of every day is waking up in the morning and finding you there beside me. It never ceases to amaze me.

BRAD. Really?

PEG. Even when I'm so angry with you I could kill you, I'm still madly in love with you. You still excite me ... after everything ... after all these years...

BRAD. Let's move back to New York. *(carressing her)* I'll excite you more there. We can get a good price for the house. And then we can travel around the world.

PEG. What are you talking about? Your job is here. We have to stay. We like it here.

BRAD. We can't afford any of this anymore.

PEG. You're exaggerating.

BRAD. Bankruptcy is sitting at our front gate.

PEG. It is not.

BRAD. We're way over our heads, Peg. My salary cut was the final blow.

PEG. What about my investments?

BRAD. Gone.

PEG. *(pause)* Gone?

BRAD. For which I take full responsibility.

PEG. Gone?

BRAD. Yes, gone. Finished. Kaput. Dead.

PEG. *(drawing away from him, sitting on the edge of the couch)* And what about the bonds?

BRAD. We sold them when we bought this house, you know that.

PEG. *All* of them?

BRAD. Yes, all of them. *(She is about to protest.)* You wanted the swimming pool, the addition to the house for your mother.

PEG. *(pause)* Oh.

BRAD. It's bad.

PEG. Well ... *(Pours herself some brandy.)* Well, I only have Mary Ellen coming in once a week now. That makes some difference. I'll cut expenses ... somehow.

BRAD. You'll have to tell Jill that we might not have her tuition for the fall.

PEG. We'll manage that.

BRAD. I'll tell her tomorrow.

PEG. We put Harriet through college—

BRAD. And look at her.

PEG. Jill *is* entitled to the same.

BRAD. She's not entitled if we don't have the money.

PEG. *(Rises.)* It will work out. It always does. Please don't say anything yet. She is working this summer.

BRAD. Be realistic.

PEG. I can ask Cammy ... if I have to.

BRAD. Do you want to start begging from your mother?

PEG. I can always go back to work.

BRAD. You haven't worked full time ... since before Harriet was born.

PEG. They like me at the hospital.

BRAD. They like you because two mornings a week you

volunteer your time. They want younger women, stronger.

PEG. I'm strong.

BRAD. Younger is what it's all about.

PEG. And you? What would your chances be back in New York? We moved here because your company said relocate or quit. You discovered *then* that the job market in New York had no use for your skills, there will be *fewer* opportunites than ever in New York.

BRAD. Well, we can stay here, my sweet wife ... and what are the prospects? What I can do in a week, a computer can do in twenty minutes. They could dump me anytime. Money would get tighter than it is now. *(Pause, pours himself more brandy.)* Of course we wouldn't have to worry about any of this if we had other income.

PEG. What other income? *(pause)* You've had too much to drink.

BRAD. You don't see where I'm headed, do you? What do we do about your mother?

PEG. I said I don't want to talk about her anymore tonight.

BRAD. We have to.

PEG. Let's go back to bed. *(Starts toward hallway.)*

BRAD. Let's get rid of your mother.

PEG. I can't put her in one of those homes. I won't.

BRAD. *(moving to her)* You don't have to, Peg. You said yourself she's acting in that same peculiar way ... just like she did before she had her stroke ... but now even more irrationally. *(pause)* She put that banana peel by her patio door. She put that dead cat in her bathtub. *(pause)* Don't you think she did?

PEG. No.

BRAD. Then who did? You?

PEG. No.

BRAD. Then who? Ahhh, I've got it, the black cat. He was eating a banana, threw the peel by her door, got inside, got sick — I don't think cats are into bananas — staggered into her bedroom, climbed into her bathtub and there expired ... just did a banana split!

PEG. *(pause)* You did those things.

BRAD. Me?

PEG. Yes.

BRAD. Yes. Me. *(Returns to his drink.)* But the woodpecker I did not get to peck on her windows. That's her own special imagination. *(Drinks.)*

PEG. *(pause)* You're drunk. This isn't you. *(Sits.)*

BRAD. The beginning of this week you told me she was chattering on about the Titanic again ... then calling you Harriet, calling you Jill. I could see that you were upset by her behavior. The next day when I came home from work you were even more upset. You told me about Cammy's woodpecker episode. I went back to the car to get the gin I'd left on the front seat, wondering what I could do to help my wife. I'd given Harry Cortesa a lift home, the slob had eaten a banana and left the peel behind. I grabbed up the gin and — I don't know why — the banana peel. So before I mixed our martinis, I went to the patio and dropped the banana peel just outside Cammy's door — I figured, what the hell! ... we might get lucky. If she had a fall she would be hospitalized and you would once again have Power-Of-Attorney ... or, hopefully, she'd simply *slip* into eternal peace. I know, I know. Obvious, stupid, amateurish! But this is a bit out of my line.

PEG. And what about the cat?

BRAD. Early Wednesday morning I came back from jogging and there was the dead black cat right by the tool shed. Had it got into the rat poison there? Who knows. You and Cammy were busy in the kitchen. I went back to the toolshed, picked up the cat by the tail, went into her bathroom and dropped it into her bathrub. That was also obvious and stupid and amateurish. She's not easily scared to death. *(pause)* Time to get professional. Get it over with once and for all.

PEG. I'm shocked.

BRAD. We need her money, we can enjoy her money. Without it, we'll be in deep trouble.

PEG. You want to end my mother's life for money?

BRAD. What's she doing with it? Bankruptcy strips you bare.

PEG. *(pause)* What do you intend to do? *(Rises.)*

BRAD. This is the perfect time ... while the girls are here. They see she's acting peculiar ... the way she behaved before her first stroke. *This* stroke, her second, will be her last.

PEG. *(pause)* What are you going to do?

BRAD. I slip into her room—

PEG. Stop.

BRAD. Pick up a pillow and—

PEG. *Stop.*

BRAD. *(Behind her, slides his arm around her waist, draws her back against him.)* Heart failure. She's eighty. No autopsy.

PEG. You are not including me in this.

BRAD. Everyone will say: "She drifted away in her sleep."

PEG. You can't do such a thing.

BRAD. I did it in Korea. Captain Bradford Campbell singlehandedly killed nine gooks ... eight he shot, one he strangled. I was a hero, I killed for my home and country. *(PEG is about to scream, and he clamps a hand over her mouth.)* I had to do it then, I have to do it now.

PEG. *(breaking from him)* No. *(pause) No.*

BRAD. How will you stop me?

PEG. I'll call the police.

BRAD. Walk into the hall. Pick up the phone. *(Long silence. She remains motionless. Finally he turns from her, retrieves his drink and downs the rest of it.)*

PEG. I love her.

BRAD. We all love our mothers.

PEG. You never liked her.

BRAD. Not much.

PEG. She likes you.

BRAD. Not much. She's a tyrant. I have never appreciated the tyranny of the old ... especially the old who are very, very rich.

PEG. I can't let you do this.

BRAD. You love this house. The garden alone makes you happy. You don't want to give it up. You don't want me to go back to New York.

PEG. *(pause)* We're nice people. *(pause)* You can't be serious.

BRAD. I'm deadly serious. *(pause)* It'll all be over in the morning, honey. It was going to happen soon anyway, you know that. We're just helping it along. *(Sits on couch.)* Right? *(Stretches back on the couch.)* Come over here. *(pause)* I'm excited, aren't you?

PEG. No.

BRAD. Aren't you? You said I still excite you so much. *You* excite me. I'm *very* excited. Come feel how excited I am...

PEG. You think sex takes care of everything.

BRAD. Hasn't it always between you and me?

PEG. *(pause)* Yes. It always has.

BRAD. Come over here. honey. We've never tried this couch.

PEG. You want to kill my mother.

BRAD. So do you.

(PEG hesitates, then turns off the LIGHT, and moves to him. MOONLIGHT spills into the room. She stands before him, he slides his hand under her nightgown, caressing her.)

BRAD. *(pause)* Come on. Get on. Ride.

PEG. No. Upstairs.

BRAD. Chicken.

PEG. Please. Upstairs.

BRAD. All right. *(He rises. They embrace, he kisses her passionately.)*

PEG. Carry me.

(He lifts her into his arms. He carries her out of the room and up the stairs. Silence. The upstairs LIGHT goes out.

Then the outside patio door is slowly opened by CAMMY. She Enters, carrying a tote bag. She closes the door quietly after her.

She sets the tote bag on the floor beside the chair. She hurries toward the hall to check if anyone is about, and again checks the patio entrance. Then she sits and from the tote bag she takes out a pistol. She cocks it. She will now wait. She is prepared.

Now the hallway LIGHT goes on. PEG comes down the stairs, enters the room, picks up the glasses and the bottle of brandy and starts back up the stairs.

PEG hesitates. CAMMY raises the pistol.

PEG sets the bottle and glasses down on an end table in the hallway, reenters the room, crosses it quickly and goes outside by the patio entrance. She does not see Cammy.

CAMMY hesitates, then moves to the patio door and looks out, still carrying the pistol. Suddenly she scurries back to the chair, aware that PEG is returning.

PEG comes back, quickly closing the patio door behind her and crosses the room. CAMMY again raises the pistol. PEG, in the hallway, retrieves the brandy bottle and the two glasses. climbs the stairs and exits. The hall LIGHT goes out.

CAMMY breathes a sigh of relief, and lowers the pistol.)

(Lights fade)

ACT II
Scene 1

SCENE: The same. Saturday. Early morning.

AT RISE: CAMMY is alone, still seated in the same spot. She is, apparently, asleep.

In a moment JILL Enters. She is wearing a nightgown. Her entrance quickly revives CAMMY.

JILL stares out at the beautiful morning, yawns, stretches, then turns to the puzzle. She tries to fit a piece, it doesn't work. She tosses it down and starts out.

CAMMY. Good morning.
JILL. *(startled)* Oh, did you scare me.
CAMMY. I'm sorry.
JILL. Ohh...
CAMMY. I didn't mean to.
JILL. *(pause)* You're up early.
CAMMY. This morning is here and I'm surprised that *I'm* here.
JILL. What did you expect?
CAMMY. Death.

JILL. *(pause)* Oh.

CAMMY. But I made it through the night. I believe that I'm safe now.

JILL. I'm having coffee and an English muffin. Do you—

CAMMY. Breakfast is at nine thirty on Saturday mornings.

JILL. Do you want anything now?

CAMMY. Yes. Would you please bring me a glass of orange juice?

JILL. Sure. *(Starts off.)*

CAMMY. Jill.

JILL. I know. "Of course," not "Sure." It doesn't matter.

CAMMY. No, no. I want to thank you for reminding me that I had this. *(Uncovers the pistol.)*

JILL. *(Pause.)* Is it loaded?

CAMMY. Of course.

JILL. *(pause)* Be careful.

CAMMY. Your grandfather taught me how to use it. He wanted me to know how to protect myself... and shoot to kill. I'm an expert shot.

JILL. You were serious last night.

CAMMY. About your father and mother trying to end my life? Oh, yes. I'm prepared now. I intend to live.

JILL. Cammy ... they're nice people. You know that.

CAMMY. I always thought so. But nice people often surprise us.

JILL. Why would they want to do such a thing?

CAMMY. My money.

JILL. You're talking about Mom and Dad.

CAMMY. You're repeating yourself.

JILL. Can I see it?

CAMMY. What?

JILL. Grampa's pistol.

CAMMY. You see it.

JILL. Can I hold it?

CAMMY. Why?

JILL. I'd like to hold it.

CAMMY. No, Harriet.

JILL. I'm Jill. *(CAMMY gives her a blank look.)* I'm Jill.

CAMMY. I know that.

JILL. You just called me Harriet.

CAMMY. Oh. Well, overlook it. You can't take this from me. It protected me through the night.

JILL. Will you be careful with it?

CAMMY. What did I just say? I was taught how to use it. Sometimes you children talk to me as if I were a two-year-old. I find that very offensive.

JILL. Just don't point it at me. *(Starts off.)*

CAMMY. If I'm not here when you get back with my orange juice I've gone squirrel hunting. *(Laughs. JILL doesn't respond. She Exits.)* She didn't think that was funny. *(Laughs again.)* I did. *(CAMMY puts the pistol into the tote bag. She's been sitting a long time. She has a little difficulty getting to her feet. Once on them she stretches a bit, picks up the tote bag and moves to the couch. She starts to lie down, changes her mind, sits. She has other plans. There is no time for sleep.)*

(HARRIET Enters, dressed, carrying an overnight bag and her purse.)

HARRIET. Good morning, Cammy.

CAMMY. Good morning, Harriet.

HARRIET. You're up early.

CAMMY. I'm always up early. We have an appointment, you know.

HARRIET. *(pause)* Oh. *(Sets down overnight bag and purse.)*

CAMMY. You haven't forgotten. You promised. You're driving me to Fenwick Florists right after breakfast. *(Manages to get to her feet, looking at the droopy African violet.)* Isn't it the saddest looking thing you've ever seen? Oh. We're both up, so we don't have to wait.

HARRIET. *(lacking enthusiasm)* No. I suppose we don't...

CAMMY. What time would they be open? Eight? Nine? Should I call? No. We can just go. We can leave now.

HARRIET. And sit outside waiting for the shop to open?

CAMMY. No. First, we'll go to that restaurant that's open twenty four hours ... the Sea Breeze. I'll treat you to a lovely breakfast and then we can exchange that atrocity that George and Myra Bentley were so kind to send to me, *not* Charles and Sarah Coleman, Charles and Sarah are dead. There. I'm quite nimble this morning. My body feels lumpy ... but my mind is clipping along, full speed. I had little sleep. *(Brings out the pistol from the tote bag.)* I sat here through the night, prepared. Just in case.

HARRIET. *(taken back)* Where did you get that?

CAMMY. It's your grandfather's. It was in the bottom of my cedar chest.

HARRIET. Bullets?

CAMMY. Of course.

HARRIET. Why don't you give it to me for safekeeping?

CAMMY. Why should I?

HARRIET. So you won't harm yourself.

CAMMY. I don't have it to harm myself, I have it to protect myself.

HARRIET. You'd better give it to me.

CAMMY. No. Take your hand away. No. My mind is very nimble this morning. Full speed. I just told you.

HARRIET. You don't want to harm yourself. Or anybody else.

CAMMY. You mean your mother and father. Well, a simple solution occurred to me just as the sun was coming up. It was as if God had whispered into my ear.

HARRIET. And what did God whisper?

CAMMY. Don't smirk, Harriet. You smirk too much — It gives your mouth an unattractive twisted look. *I said* it was *as if* God had whispered into my ear, I didn't say He *did* ... I have thought of a way to prevent harm to myself and harm to others. *(Sits.)* After we exchange the African violet we can go to see Bruce Walker in Westerly. Your parents are represented here by Everett Duncan; I prefer young Bruce, he's more amiable and, frankly, I know he needs my business. Also, he is the grandson of an old friend. Bruce Walker the First, his grandfather, and his dizzy wife Ethel — Oh, she was a dizzy-do — had a summer place next to ours in Southampton when your mother was a child, and—

HARRIET. You're rambling, Cammy.

CAMMY. I am not rambling. I am making a slight detour, and I am aware of it.

HARRIET. Cammy, get—

CAMMY. *Anyway*, the reason we are going to see Bruce Walker the Third is to change my will. I had left everything to your mother.

HARRIET. And now you want to change all that and leave it to charity.

CAMMY. No. I'll leave it to my granddaughters ... equally divided between you and Jill.

HARRIET. *(pause)* I approve of that.

CAMMY. I thought you would. By changing my will, I'll stop them. They are trying to kill me for my money.

HARRIET. Of course.

CAMMY. I fear it's *both* of them.

HARRIET. And if you remove Mother from your will no one will hurt you.

CAMMY. Why didn't I think of it sooner? I asked myself that question. And the answer was: Because I didn't want to believe that it could be true. I thought they loved me ... in their fashion. *(pause)* At least your mother. *(pause)* And when we return, after our morning excursion, I must make other plans in regard to the future.

HARRIET. Such as what?

CAMMY. *(Rises.)* First things first. I'll change. I have a new summer hat. I want to wear a hat this morning. *(Starts off, hesitates.)* You do believe me now, don't you?

HARRIET. Oh, yes. But I think there's a problem. It's Saturday...

CAMMY. I'm ahead of you. Bruce Walker is in his office

on Saturday mornings; he's only been in Westerly a short time. *(Starts off again.)* Then we'll make a final stop at the bank. *(Hesitates.)* How much money did you want to borrow?

HARRIET. Three ... *four* thousand dollars.

CAMMY. *(Chuckles.)* I'll lend it to you.

HARRIET. I accept.

CAMMY. Of course.

HARRIET. Thank you.

CAMMY. You're welcome.

HARRIET. Hurry.

CAMMY. I will. *(Exits into her room. HARRIET is still. She smiles. Things have taken a decided turn for the better. She begins to glow, then laughs, then happily hums a current song, even dances a little.)*

(JILL returns with a tray with coffee, English muffins and orange juice.)

HARRIET. Good morning, sister dear.

JILL. What are you doing up so early? Were you going back to New York without saying goodbye or anything?

HARRIET. Would I do that?

JILL. Yes. *(Sits at coffee table.)*

HARRIET. Cammy was already up and reminding me that I'd promised to do her a favor.

JILL. Where is she?

HARRIET. Getting dressed. Is this for her?

JILL. Just the juice. The rest is mine. *(HARRIET takes the juice.)* No. Get your own.

HARRIET. *(quickly drinks some of it)* She's taking me out to breakfast at the Sea Breeze and then I will chauffeur her on to Fenwick Florists so she—

JILL. Did you see the pistol?

HARRIET. Yes.

JILL. It's loaded.

HARRIET. She says it is. *(grandly)* She has it for protection.

JILL. We have to get it away from her before she hurts herself ... or us.

HARRIET. I'll take care of it.

JILL. Should I wake up Mom and Dad?

HARRIET. No. Let them sleep. I'll take care of it. Relax.

JILL. Is she getting senile?

HARRIET. Let's just say ... a little tilted.

JILL. She told me she was going squirrel hunting.

HARRIET. She *is* a little squirrelly.

JILL. They'll have to put her in one of those homes, won't they?

HARRIET. Maybe.

JILL. That'll finish her off fast. She's so used to having her own way. Change would kill her.

HARRIET. Such concern.

JILL. She's eighty years old. I don't think you care much about her.

HARRIET. You don't like her either.

JILL. I like her ... spirit. And she was always nice to me, she took me everywhere when I was a kid. Oh, she's snobby and bossy and old fashioned ... but who else has a grandmother who's met Mark Twain and Amelia

Earhart and President Roosevelt and—

HARRIET. I know the list. *(Goes and gets her purse, and through the following applies make-up.)*

JILL. Well, I'm still impressed. Cammy's ... history. *(Begins to cry.)*

HARRIET. *(pause)* Oh, Jill...

JILL. *(pause)* I can't help it.

HARRIET. She's a silly old peacock.

JILL. You don't feel anything about anything.

HARRIET. And you are such a marshmallow.

JILL. You don't.

HARRIET. Drink your coffee.

JILL. It's not only Cammy. It's Mom, too.

HARRIET. Hopefully, we won't have to put *her* away for awhile.

JILL. Oh, shut up. She's worried, I can tell ... about Cammy ... money ... she slept in the den last night. She and Dad must've had a fight.

HARRIET. If they had a fight it wasn't about Cammy or money ... it was about Kay Tobin. Dear old Dad is screwing around with her again.

JILL. Why do you always think the worst of him?

HARRIET. Where were you during dinner last night? That phone call from her got him all puffed up and strutting again. He's almost as vain as Cammy.

JILL. *(firmly)* They've been happy here since we moved from New York.

HARRIET. You're observant.

JILL. They have been.

HARRIET. He's never liked it here, he just puts up a front. *She* likes it here. She thinks she can keep a better eye on him.

JILL. You don't want anybody to be happy. You love misery.

HARRIET. This morning I'm *very* happy. Doesn't it show?

JILL. That's a fake smile.

HARRIET. Do you want to know why I'm happy?

JILL. Cammy must be giving you some money.

HARRIET. Ask me.

JILL. You called Michael in New York and he'll take you back.

HARRIET. Say: "Why are you happy, Harriet?"

JILL. "Why are you happy, Harriet?"

HARRIET. It's a secret.

JILL. You always did that. I could punch you.

HARRIET. I'll tell you later. I promise.

JILL. *(sudden revelation)* Is something up with Cammy? *(pause)* Last night you were ready to drown her.

HARRIET. I'm going to treat her as if she were ... the Queen of England. Imagine Cammy as the Queen of England. For once I will be the dutiful granddaughter ... like you.

JILL. What are you scheming?

(CAMMY returns, changed, with hat and glove accessories.)

CAMMY. I'm ready. Wasn't I quick?

HARRIET. Like lightning.

JILL. Harriet drank your orange juice.

CAMMY. Orange juice? Oh. Oh, yes.

HARRIET. Forgive me.

CAMMY. Don't be silly. I'll have some freshly squeezed

at the Sea Breeze.

JILL. I love your hat.

CAMMY. Thank you. Isn't it nice? I love it, too. Goodbye, Jill. We're off.

JILL. Have fun.

CAMMY. It is going to be such a beautiful day. I'm not afraid anymore. *(impulsively kisses JILL)*

JILL. You *are* in a good mood.

CAMMY. Oh, yes. *(to HARRIET:)* Ready, Jill?

HARRIET. I'm Harriet, she's Jill.

CAMMY. I know, I know. That's a natural mistake. I know. *(and they start off)*

JILL. Hey! The African violet.

HARRIET. Oh, yes. That's what this trip is all about, isn't it? *(JILL has grabbed up the plant, handing it to HARRIET.)*

CAMMY. Hay is for horses. You just said: "Hey, the African violet." I said: "Hay is for—

JILL. Hey, Cammy, bring me back a treat.

CAMMY. What am I to do with you?

JILL. Hey! Stay loose, it's okay.

HARRIET. Cammy, where's the pistol?

CAMMY. In my bag.

HARRIET. Give it to Jill. You won't be needing it.

CAMMY. *(pause)* I suppose I won't now. But why can't I take it with me?

HARRIET. You don't need it anymore. Give it to Jill. *(CAMMY removes it from the tote bag, gives it to JILL.)*

CAMMY. Put it in a safe place until I get back. Bye.

HARRIET. Bye.

JILL. Bye.

(CAMMY chatters inaudibly as she and HARRIET Exit. JILL awkwardly holds the pistol. She gets her coffee and sits at the puzzle table. She sets down the coffee mug and the pistol. But the pistol makes her uneasy. She suddenly covers it with the puzzle box cover. PEG Enters the hallway in her nightgown and light robe. She hesitates by the stairs, and then comes into the room.)

PEG. Good morning, Jill.

JILL. Morning, Mom.

PEG. *(pause)* You never liked puzzles much.

JILL. I like Mark Twain's face. He has character.

PEG. I saw Harriet and Cammy drive off. Where are they going?

JILL. First to the Sea Breeze for breakfast ... and then to Fenwicks to wage war.

PEG. Good.

JILL. Look. She had Grampa's pistol. *(Uncovers it.)* For protection. From you and Dad.

PEG. Oh.

JILL. I think she sat up all night in here.

PEG. *(as she picks up the pistol)* I'm surprised she didn't take it with her. *(Points the pistol, impersonating CAMMY.)* "Mr. Fenwick, you've cheated me. Give me the best you've got or prepare for eternity."

JILL. *(Laughs.)* She'd come back with every flower in the store.

PEG. Or ... all of his rose bushes. I could do a lot with Fenwick's rose bushes. *(in reference to the pistol)* She must've had this in her cedar chest.

JILL. Does it shake you up? All her dopey murder talk.

PEG. *(crossing away from her)* Yes.

JILL. *(pause)* You won't have to put her in one of those homes for the whatever, will you?

PEG. I hope not.

JILL. What does Dad think?

PEG. We've discussed it.

JILL. And?

PEG. We can't have her going around threatening us with this.

JILL. Harriet says she's getting tilted.

PEG. So's Harriet.

JILL. *(Laughs.)* Uh huh. *(pause)* I hope you and Dad can figure out something. When you're eighty years old, you should have family around you. Don't you think so? *(pause)* I think she'll come out of it ... all that dopey talk. I have that feeling. *(pause)* I do.

PEG. Why are you staring at me like that?

JILL. The older Cammy gets ... the older you get ... the older I get.

PEG. *(setting down the pistol)* Have no fear. I'll never be a burden to you.

JILL. Is that what she's become? She can be a real pain in the ass, I know ... but a burden? You two always got along.

PEG. Barely.

JILL. You love her.

PEG. I've never liked her much.

JILL. But do you love her.

PEG. *(pause)* She's my mother.

JILL. You do love her.

PEG. I suppose ... in a way. *(Sits on couch.)* But daughters aren't required to love their mothers.

JILL. Oh, no?

PEG. Do you love me?

JILL. Sure.

PEG. How nice.

JILL. *(joining her on the couch)* Do you love me?

PEG. You know I do. *(Hugs her.)*

JILL. You're upset about Cammy, aren't you. I know ... it's a hard decision.

PEG. *(pause)* Your grandmother, with all her idiosyncracies, is a very brave woman. When your grandfather found out he had incurable cancer, he was devastated. That big strapping man ... over two hundred pounds ... and he wound up weighing eighty five. Well, she would not let him end up in any hospital ... or have any nurse hovering about him. She told the doctors that she would take care of him and she did. And every day ... except in the worst weather ... she would walk with him in Central Park ... and then, when he grew weaker, she pushed him in a wheelchair. That went on for almost two years. She never complained, not once. "He made my life happy," she said. "I will give him all the love and attention he deserves until he breathes his last."

JILL. *(sitting up)* What's that got to do with now?

PEG. She took care of her own. Isn't she entitled to the same? We should give her a place here ... forever ... no matter how much it may inconvenience us. You're right, Jill. I would never put her away. *(Rises, picks up pistol from the coffee table.)* One must protect oneself.

JILL. Will you put the gun down. Put it down, Mom, please.

PEG. *(Sets it down.)* There. Feel better?

JILL. Yes.

PEG. I need some Vitamin C.

JILL. *(as PEG starts off)* Are you going to jog this morning?

PEG. No. This morning I'm going to be bad.

JILL. And Dad?

PEG. I think he'll be bad, too. *(Starts off again, returns, picks up the tray and again starts out.)*

JILL. How come you slept downstairs in the den last night?

PEG. Oh, your father was restless ... not feeling too well. We both had a little too much brandy last night.

JILL. Nothing to do with Kay Tobin?

PEG. That was over and done with three years ago.

JILL. You forgave him.

PEG. Don't pry.

JILL. Did you?

PEG. *(pause)* It took time.

JILL. Harriet hasn't forgiven him.

PEG. Harriet has a difficult time forgiving anybody anything. And it was none of her business.

JILL. But why did Kay Tobin call here last night?

PEG. Your father told us. She wanted a letter of recommendation.

JILL. Was that all?

PEG. If you want details ask him. If I don't get some orange juice, I will die. *(Exits. JILL sits quietly for a moment, sips her coffee. Now she turns and looks at the pistol, rises, crosses to the coffee table, carefully picks up the pistol and puts it into an obscure drawer. JILL Exits.)*

(LIGHT pinpoints the drawer where the pistol has been placed. Then the lights fade.)

Scene 3

SCENE: The same. Around 12 noon.

AT RISE: The room is empty. In a moment HARRIET, now wearing sun glasses, Enters. She is carrying a bonsai tree. She is followed by CAMMY.

CAMMY. The house is so quiet.

HARRIET. *(looking out the window)* Jill is by the pool ... Mother is busybusybusy in her garden.

CAMMY. Your father isn't there reading the paper?

HARRIET. No.

CAMMY. He's gone golfing. *(And she sits in the chair at the puzzle table. HARRIET sets down the new plant.)* It's certainly more beautiful than any African violet isn't it? I want to show them the bonsai tree ... and I want to tell them what I've done. I have guaranteed myself a life that will end in a normal fashion. I can live the rest of my days without fear.

HARRIET. *(removing her sun glasses)* Do you want me to get them?

CAMMY. Yes, please. *(And having obviously overextended herself, a deep sigh escapes her. She is in need of sleep.)*

HARRIET. *(pause)* Are you all right?

CAMMY. *(lightly)* A bit tired. Other than that, I'm fine. *(HARRIET Exits by the patio door. CAMMY begins to remove the glove from her left hand. It is painful. Her arthritis is bothering her.)* Too much excitement this morning, missy. A little too much. *(Begins to prepare herself. Sits more upright. But it is an effort. Looking down at the puzzle.)* Well, Mark Twain, is there life after death? You know, but you won't tell. Nobody ever does.

(PEG Enters followed by HARRIET.)

PEG. Are you all right? Harriet said—

CAMMY. I am fine.

PEG. *(seeing the bonsai tree)* Oh, look.

CAMMY. *(overlapping)* I may have overextended myself a little ... but I'll soon be taking a nap. Harriet and I had quite an adventurous morning. We had a delicious breakfast at the Sea Breeze ... it was high tide, the waves were glorious ... and that was followed by a nice drive to Fenwick Florists—

PEG. And you got quite a replacement. *(Removes work gloves, sets them down.)*

CAMMY. Isn't it beautiful?

PEG. Yes, it is. Were you cantankerous at Fenwicks?

CAMMY. I was very demure.

PEG. Demure?

CAMMY. Well ... *(HARRIET laughs.)*

(JILL Enters.)

PEG. Look, Jill.

JILL. Oh, wow! For the African violet?

CAMMY. Of course.

JILL. Oh, Cammy, you character. What is it?

HARRIET. A bonsai tree, dummy.

JILL. Expensive?

HARRIET. The most expensive one in the store.

PEG. Good.

JILL. What did you do? Tell me.

CAMMY. I was a perfect lady.

PEG. Demure.

HARRIET. She was not. *(They all laugh.)*

CAMMY. Harriet goaded me on. I told Mr. Fenwick I was shocked by the abomination.

JILL. Abomination! *(Applauds.)*

HARRIET. There were three other customers. She showed each of them, very closely—

CAMMY. —the abomination. Mr. Fenwick did not appreciate that.

HARRIET. He was intimidated by her hat.

CAMMY. And my gloves. Gloves can do that.

JILL. Oh, I wish I'd been there.

CAMMY. Mr. Fenwick told me to choose whatever I wanted. Once I chose it, he almost reneged.

HARRIET. But the three customers—

CAMMY. Whom I'd never seen before...

HARRIET. —applauded her choice.

CAMMY. It pays to complain when you've been—

JILL. Taken.

PEG. You were always good at complaining—

CAMMY. Are you criticizing me?

PEG. No, you always did complain when you'd been—

JILL. Taken.

PEG. Yes.

CAMMY. Well, this time around I did not find it necessary to raise my voice, Peg. I didn't.

HARRIET. She didn't ... a demure lady.

CAMMY. Oh, demure, yes ... but dangerous. *(again they all laugh)*

PEG. *(starting off)* Do you want some lunch?

CAMMY. No, nothing. I had such a big breakfast. What I need is a nap. *(Rises, gathers up her bag and gloves and hat.)* I got so little sleep last night. I was wide awake, waiting ... for you or Brad.

PEG. You wasted your time, didn't you?

CAMMY. Jill, where is my pistol?

JILL. You said put it in a safe place. I did.

CAMMY. Oh. Well, never mind. I don't need it anymore. Now I have *better* protection. Where is Brad? Playing golf?

PEG. Earlier he wasn't feeling well. He may still be sleeping.

CAMMY. It's almost noon.

PEG. Or he may have gone golfing. I've been in the garden most of the morning. He doesn't tell me everywhere he goes.

HARRIET. *(to CAMMY:)* Do you want me to see if he's still upstairs?

CAMMY. No, it's not necessary. Peg's here. *(pause)* After we stopped at Fenwicks and settled that issue ... well, after that ... I had Harriet drive me to see Bruce Walker in Westerly. *(Waits for a response.)*

PEG. *(pause)* Go on.

CAMMY. *(victorious)* I drew up a new will. He had me dictate it to his secretary. She typed it up in no time. It took less than half an hour. Remarkable. The old will left everything to you, Peg. The new will divides everything equally between Harriet and Jill.

JILL. What?

HARRIET. You heard her.

JILL. Why did you do that?

CAMMY. To protect myself.

JILL. Mom and Dad wouldn't hurt a fly. It's all your imagination.

CAMMY. Then I am on the safe side of my imagination. It can take a rest. *(PEG laughs.)* You find it amusing?

PEG. Oh, yes.

CAMMY. I don't. Harriet doesn't either.

PEG. I'm sure Harriet wouldn't. *(pause, more to HARRIET)* You have had a busy morning.

HARRIET. I was just being helpful.

PEG. Turning me into a pauper.

CAMMY. I have done what was necessary. Now we can ... we can—

PEG. Resume our daily living?

CAMMY. Exactly. I desperately need a nap. I must sleep. We can talk later in the day.

PEG. Yes, we'll have to.

CAMMY. *(moving toward her door)* I did it to protect myself. You must understand that. You must convey that to Brad.

HARRIET. She has obstructed *irrational behavior.*

CAMMY. Exactly. Thank you for everything, Harriet.

HARRIET. You're most welcome, Cammy.

CAMMY. *(to all:)* Have a pleasant afternoon. I intend to sleep through most of it. *(Exits into her room.)*

HARRIET. *(Long pause. Gets a brush from her purse, brushes her hair.)* I am now so grateful that I came home to celebrate my dear, sweet grandmother's eightieth birthday.

JILL. A will can be changed ... just like that?

HARRIET. Just like that. You and I get everything ... when Cammy departs for places unknown.

JILL. She'll live to be a hundred.

HARRIET. Maybe.

PEG. But you hope not.

HARRIET. I had no idea that she wanted to change her will until this morning.

PEG. And immediately you encouraged her.

HARRIET. You told me to be nice to her. So I obliged you.

PEG. New wills can be changed, too.

HARRIET. And to think that you wouldn't lend me any money. *(to JILL:)* Not one penny. Mean, uncaring, self-centered parents. My father the heartbreaker ... my mother the heart*acher.* Sound accurate?

PEG. I never realized you were so contemptuous of us.

HARRIET. Dear Dad. I hope he's still upstairs. I must tell him the good news. He'll be overjoyed. *(Starts off, hesitates.)* I'm going to be rich. You, too Jill. You, Mother dear, are going to be ... not rich. *(is on her way)* Why, someday you might need to come begging to me. I'll look forward to that. *(Exits upstairs, long silence.)*

JILL. Harriet could've stopped her. *(pause)* Can't you call that lawyer? — What's his name?

PEG. Bruce Walker the Third.

JILL. Can't you call him?

PEG. Why?

JILL. Call him and tell him that Cammy's been acting ... weird?

PEG. I believe that Cammy was in full command of her faculties this morning.

JILL. What are you going to do?

PEG. *(picking up her work gloves)* I'm going back outside and work on my geraniums.

JILL. Aren't you going to call that lawyer?

(HARRIET comes running down the stairs.)

HARRIET. Come quick! Something's wrong with Dad. I tried to wake him ... I think he's dead! Come quick! *(JILL follows quickly after HARRIET. Then PEG, more slowly, starts after them.)*

(In a moment CAMMY returns by way of her room.)

CAMMY. *(as she Enters, carrying a small paper bag)* Jill! Jill, I forgot before. You asked for a treat. I brought you one. *(PEG, on the stairs, stops at the sound of her mother's voice, and turns to her. CAMMY cannot see PEG.)* Where have they gone?

(Lights fade.)

ACT III
Scene 1

SCENE: The same. Later that day. Mid-afternoon.

AT RISE: PEG is seated at the puzzle table. Occasionally she fits a piece of the puzzle. HARRIET sits on the couch. Occasionally she glances through a magazine set on a pillow beside her. JILL is wandering aimlessly about the room.

JILL. *(long pause)* Why is Inspector Connors talking to each of us?

PEG. *(pause)* It's routine.

HARRIET. *(with a slight flourish)* Maybe he thinks Dad died in an unorthodox fashion.

JILL. It was a heart attack. Doctor Potter said so.

PEG. It's routine. It has to be done.

JILL. *(long pause)* I still can't believe it.

PEG. Sit down, Jill.

JILL. He won't make much sense out of Cammy. She seems so out of it. *(pause)* Don't you think so, Mom?

PEG. Sit down.

JILL. *(Sits, then is instantly up.)* I don't want to.

HARRIET. Candy?

JILL. No.

HARRIET. Candy kiss, Mom?

PEG. No, thank you.

JILL. I don't see why he's questioning us all *separately.*

HARRIET. *(eating a candy kiss)* He's doing his job.

PEG. He'll be gone soon.

JILL. I still don't understand.

HARRIET. *(snappishly)* You don't have to.

JILL. Be quiet.

HARRIET. *(pause, to PEG:)* Is there a will?

JILL. Why don't you shut up?

HARRIET. Is there?

PEG. Yes.

HARRIET. Insurance?

PEG. Yes.

HARRIET. *(pause)* And?...

PEG. Sorry, Harriet. Your father left everything to me. I have no intention of letting you borrow any of it. It will not be a great deal of money.

HARRIET. Oh, my immediate problem is solved. Cammy let me borrow the money from her.

PEG. *(pause)* You *did* have a busy morning. *(HARRIET eats another candy kiss.)*

(CAMMY Entering. A sweater over her shoulders.)

CAMMY. Inspector Connors wants to speak with you, Jill. *(JILL Exits, pause.)* He's very nice, isn't he, Peg?

PEG. Yes.

CAMMY. Very nice for an Irishman. *(pause)* Often the Irish have that overbearing manner about them, too hearty, too cheerful. This one's manner is refreshing. Very straight forward. *(to HARRIET:)* Why are you eating those candy kisses? They're Jill's treat.

HARRIET. I told you in the store that candy kisses were *my* favorite, not Jill's.

CAMMY. Oh, yes, it *was* you: "Cammy, candy kisses."

HARRIET. Me. Just a slip of a girl.

CAMMY. Yes. Not Jill, oh, yes, *you.* You couldn't pronounce Grammy. And I liked Cammy. *(pause, moving about PEG)* Inspector Connors said he'd played golf with Brad. Did you know that, Peg? He said when he played with him that Brad got a hole-in-one. That's exceptional. He said he always thought that Brad was in good physical condition, but I said once you pass fifty there are no guarantees ... as far as one's health is concerned. *(pause)* Oh, I told him about the woodpecker I heard tapping on my windows earlier this week. He believed me. But I said nothing about the banana peel or the black cat ... or any of that. *(pause)* Not a word. *(pause, sits)* Are the funeral arrangements taken care of?

PEG. Yes.

CAMMY. When will the service be?

PEG. Tuesday.

HARRIET. Will he be cremated?

PEG. Yes. That's what he wanted.

CAMMY. I don't want to be cremated ... when my time comes.

PEG. I know that, Mother.

CAMMY. I want to be buried alongside my beloved Brad.

HARRIET. *(attempting to restrain a laugh)* Oh, my God.

CAMMY. What?

HARRIET. You just said alongside Brad.

CAMMY. I did? Oh. I meant my beloved Jeffrey. I'm sorry, Peg.

HARRIET. *(to PEG:)* Will there be an autopsy?

PEG. *(pause)* No.

HARRIET. Why not?

PEG. Why should there be?

HARRIET. Inspector Connors seemed to think there would be.

PEG. I didn't get that impression.

HARRIET. *I* did.

PEG. Dr. Potter said your father died of natural causes. That's the end of it.

CAMMY. *(Rises, moving about but still very near to PEG.)* There we were at Fenwick Florists this morning, Harriet ... and we didn't think then, did we ... how could we? ... we didn't know. Now Fenwick will have so many orders for floral bouquets of sympathy ... for your father. *(pause)* The bonsai tree is lovely, isn't it? It was a perfect exchange.

PEG. Why don't you lie down?

CAMMY. You should have changed to talk to Inspector Connors. Your garden clothes are inappropriate.

PEG. I don't think he cares about what I'm wearing.

CAMMY. He said he liked my dress.

PEG. Good.

CAMMY. You had time to change. *(no response)* Oh, I understand. You were planning on gardening more this afternoon. *(pause)* But you won't be able to. It's getting so cloudy ... and cooler. It's supposed to storm. This morning when Harriet and I were driving along we were listening to the radio. The weather report said thunderstorms later in the afternoon and into the night. We discussed it. Such a beautiful morning. Not a cloud in the sky. We agreed that the weatherman must be wrong. But now it's cloudy and cooler. He was right. *(Drained, sits by HARRIET on the couch. Pause. Sits back.)* Harriet, I know we talked about the possibility of my returning to New York to live with you ... but I need to be here with my daughter. She needs me now. *(pause)* It would've been nice if you'd changed, Peg. Your blue silk would've been appropriate. But I'm sure Inspector Connors understands, too. *(pause, beginning to drift off)* I said nothing about the pistol. I said nothing about the banana peel ... and the cat. I said nothing about ... murder. *(Drifts off to sleep. PEG looks over to her. In a moment she rises and takes an afghan off the back of the couch. HARRIET rises and lifts CAMMY'S feet onto the couch. PEG covers CAMMY with the afghan.)*

HARRIET. *(pause)* How are you feeling?

PEG. Do you care?

HARRIET. I asked.

PEG. *(moving away from the couch)* I feel numb.

HARRIET. That will pass.

PEG. Probably. *(pause)* What was that all about?

HARRIET. What?

PEG. Cammy ... saying she was going to live with you.

HARRIET. We talked about it this morning.

PEG. *(Chuckles.)* How long do you think that would last?

HARRIET. I'm willing.

PEG. As long as she pays well for her keep.

HARRIET. She pays you well for her keep.

PEG. You'd live with her just to make sure that she didn't change that will.

HARRIET. Aren't you supposed to be in mourning or shock or in tears?

PEG. You always were greedy.

HARRIET. From the time I can remember, I've heard that kind of remark from you. *(pause)* Will you contact Kay Tobin?

PEG. *(pause)* Why should I?

HARRIET. She's waiting for a letter of recommendation. Isn't she? Or would you prefer to let her stumble across the notice in the obituary column?

PEG. Stumble.

HARRIET. Wouldn't it be kinder to contact her?

PEG. You do it ... if you choose to.

HARRIET. I don't think it's my place.

PEG. *(flaring)* Do as you please!

(JILL returns. She has been crying again.)

JILL. He's leaving now, Mom. He wants to see you again.

PEG. Fine. *(PEG hesitates, JILL hugs her. They comfort one another. PEG Exits.)*

JILL. Is Cammy asleep?

HARRIET. Yes.

JILL. I started crying again, I couldn't stop. I just can't believe he's dead. Dad was never sick.

HARRIET. No, he wasn't...

JILL. Mom's handling it well. So brave.

HARRIET. Isn't she?

JILL. We should do everything we can to make it easier for her.

HARRIET. I wonder what really happened.

JILL. *(overlapping)* You're *not,* you know.

HARRIET. Cammy almost had me convinced that they were, somehow, trying to do her in.

JILL. Will you—

HARRIET. She was coming to New York to live with me. To get away from them. Now she's changed her mind. She says she's going to stay with her daughter. Why?

JILL. Why wouldn't she? Mom's alone. And you and Cammy living together? You wouldn't last three days.

HARRIET. You can tolerate a helluva lot when there are goodies around the corner. She made a new will this morning, remember? Everything is left to you and me. If she stays here, mother will manage to get that new will changed back to its original form.

JILL. Is that all you can think about right now?

HARRIET. Six million dollars is a lot to think about.

JILL. Our father just died.

HARRIET. Too bad it wasn't Cammy instead.

JILL. *Where are your feelings?!*

HARRIET. Shhhh, Cammy's sleeping. Sleep, Cammy, sleep ... forever, never wake up. I'd have three million, you'd have three million—

JILL. Shut up.

HARRIET. I could walk right over there now, take one of those pillows—

JILL. *Shut up!*

HARRIET. Shhh. You'll wake her. *(pause)* Sure you don't want a candy kiss?

JILL. You eat them, all of them. Stuff yourself... maybe you'll choke to death.

HARRIET. Nasty.

JILL. Didn't you love him at all?

HARRIET. You know I didn't!

JILL. Well, I did.

HARRIET. You're a dummy.

(PEG returns.)

PEG. Well, he's gone. *(pause)* He is a nice man. Your father told me he enjoyed playing golf with him. *(moving near JILL who is by the puzzle table)* Mark Twain is almost finished. Cammy will be pleased. All we have left is the top of his head. Oh, I think that one may fit. The one under your thumb.

JILL. Oh.

PEG. That one.

JILL. Oh. *(pause)* You're right.

PEG. Good.

HARRIET. I'd better call my office and tell them I won't be back until Wednesday.

PEG. Are they open on Saturdays?

HARRIET. No. The answering service. Oh, I don't have anything black here.

PEG. I'm sure you can find something in Westerly... or the Mall.

HARRIET. Yes. I'll do that later.

PEG. Good.

HARRIET. You can come shopping with me, Jill.

JILL. I have a black dress upstairs.

HARRIET. You can still come with me.

JILL. I don't want to. *(pause)* Isn't it funny? *(moving toward the hallway)* I'm hungry.

HARRIET. So am I. What are you going to get?

JILL. I don't know.

PEG. There's plenty of roast beef from last night. And there's tuna fish. You love tuna fish.

JILL. Come on, Mom.

PEG. No. *(Again sits at the puzzle table.)* I just want to sit here and work the puzzle ... and keep an eye on your grandmother. She's had so little sleep. She'll be all turned around when she wakes up.

JILL. Can I bring you something?

PEG. Tea would be nice.

JILL. And an English muffin?

PEG. All right. *(as JILL starts off)* Jill, where did you put the pistol?

JILL. In the drawer ... there. Why?

PEG. I'll put it in a safe place ... without the bullets.

JILL. Do you want me to do it now?

PEG. No. I'll take care of it. *(JILL starts out, returns, hugs her mother from behind.)*

JILL. I know how much you loved him. *(pause)* Me, too. *(Kisses her mother's head, begins to cry again and quickly Exits.)*

PEG. *(Begins to work the puzzle again. Long pause.)* I thought you were going to call New York.

HARRIET. I am. *(pause)* I'm going to make three calls. My office, Michael...

PEG. And Kay Tobin.

HARRIET. Yes.

PEG. *(pause)* Good.

HARRIET. I'll charge the calls to my home phone number.

PEG. You don't have to do that.

HARRIET. I will though. Dad didn't leave you much ... and Cammy has changed her will. You'd better watch your pennies ... if you want to go on living here ... in your nice house ... with your nice garden. *(pause)* He *was* seeing her again, you know.

PEG. *(pause)* Does it matter now?

HARRIET. He always had something on the side.

PEG. *(Rises, angry.) That's not true.*

HARRIET. *Bullshit.*

PEG. Go and make your phone calls.

HARRIET. *(pause)* Stupid woman. *(Exits.)*

(PEG is shaken. she restrains a cry of agony and with a swift gesture sweeps the puzzle off the table. This sound awakens CAMMY. In a moment PEG starts across the room.)

CAMMY. I know, you know. *(PEG hesitates.)* While I was sitting in the living room talking to Inspector Connors it all came clear to me. *(Manages to sit up.)* Last night I came in here to the sun room because I thought it was a good safe place to be. I sat here, holding the pistol, waiting in the dark for you and Brad. You came in here and picked up the bottle of brandy and the glasses and started out and in the hall set them down and you came back in and went directly outside, you didn't see me. You were *out there ... I watched ...* and then you came back. You walked so close to me. If you'd looked at me, if you'd discovered me there, I'm sure I would have fired the pistol. I thought you meant to harm me. *(PEG turns to her.)* Now I know you didn't.

(A shadow appears in the hallway, then we see it's HARRIET. She overhears the following.)

CAMMY. You went outside and you went into that tool shed and you got that poison you have to keep the rodents away. Then you came back into this room, so close to me, and you went back upstairs with the brandy and the glasses and somehow you put that poison into his brandy. You did that because you knew he was going to end my life. Instead, it was his life that ended in the night. *(pause)* You saved my life. *(pause)* I should've known. You wouldn't let any harm come to me. *(HARRIET Exits.)* I'll tear up that new will.

PEG. It doesn't matter.

CAMMY. *(pause)* Please forgive me. Forgive your mother. *(PEG moves to her, takes her hand, comforts her. Pause.)* Poor Mark Twain. He's all over the floor.

PEG. He'll survive. *(PEG helps CAMMY to lie back again and covers her with the afghan.)*

CAMMY. You'll take care of me?

PEG. Shhhhhhhh.

CAMMY. Forever?

PEG. Go to sleep.

CAMMY. I said nothing about the pistol. I said nothing about the banana peel and the cat. I said nothing about murder.

(HARRIET returns.)

HARRIET. I didn't make my New York calls yet, Mother. I called the police. When Inspector Connors gets back to his office, he'll find my message.

CAMMY. What is she saying?

PEG. Sleep.

HARRIET. *(pause)* Well?

PEG. I loved your father. I love your grandmother. *(pause)* Make your other calls, Harriet. *(In a moment HARRIET Exits. PEG gently moves aside a strand of hair from her mother's face. Then she crosses the room, opens a drawer, takes out the pistol, crosses to the patio door and Exits. Silence.)*

(Then there is a pistol SHOT from offstage.)

(Lights fade.)

Scene 2

SCENE: That evening. (It has been raining.)

AT RISE: JILL Enters. She sets down her shoulder bag, and then takes off a windbreaker. She stares at the doorway leading onto the patio. Then she turns away.

(HARRIET Enters, carrying a mug of coffee.)

HARRIET. Any trouble at the gate?

JILL. Not really. There were two policemen.

HARRIET. Those reporters and TV people are still there.

JILL. Yes.

HARRIET. Did they bother you at the hospital?

JILL. Not much.

HARRIET. How's Cammy?

JILL. I left her sleeping.

HARRIET. She didn't have a stroke?

JILL. *(pause)* You sound disappointed.

HARRIET. How is she? What did Dr. Potter think?

JILL. They'll be doing tests in the morning. He said she's a tough old bird. *(Kneels down and begins to pick up the scattered puzzle.)*

HARRIET. She is. And we thought she was tilted.

JILL. You thought she was.

HARRIET. You don't have to do that.

JILL. I want to.

HARRIET. Then do it. *(pause)* I called their lawyer, Everett Duncan. He came right over. He's the executor.

JILL. You're very efficient.

HARRIET. Jill, you've been at the hospital for four hours. This place has been ... bedlam. It made sense to get as much cleared up as soon as possible. He'll be back tomorrow to go over everything with both of us. They were in debt. We won't wind up with very much.

JILL. I don't want to talk about money now. *(Sits at puzzle table.)*

HARRIET. He was very helpful. He and Inspector Connors were handling everything. *(pause)* There will be a hearing...

JILL. *(pause)* You read the newspapers ... this kind of thing happens to other people.

HARRIET. *(pause)* There'll be an autopsy, too, you know. Dad's. It has to be done.

JILL. Last night I was celebrating my grandmother's eightieth birthday. Tonight she's in the hospital. My father is dead. My mother is dead. And I can't cry anymore.

HARRIET. *(pause)* Michael is coming.

JILL. He is?

HARRIET. *(setting down her coffee mug)* On the ten o'clock train. I guess he still cares.

JILL. Or thinks you might become rich.

HARRIET. *(pause)* That crossed my mind. *(pause)* Did you get something to eat?

JILL. No.

HARRIET. Michael will be hungry when he gets here. Well, there's plenty of roast beef from last night. And the birthday cake. He loves chocolate cake. Michael can eat anything and not gain an ounce. I envy him. *(pause)* Fix yourself something to eat.

JILL. *(Rises.)* I'm going to take a shower and go back to the hospital.

HARRIET. Why?

JILL. I want to be there when she wakes up.

HARRIET. You'll be hounded by reporters and those awful TV people.

JILL. I can take care of myself. Bruce Walker said if I needed him to call.

HARRIET. *(pause)* When did you talk to him?

JILL. He saw the six o'clock news. He came to the hospital to see if he could help in any way.

HARRIET. Concerned about losing his wealthy client.

JILL. He likes Cammy.

HARRIET. Of course. *(as JILL starts off)* Jill. Your jacket.

JILL. What about it?

HARRIET. Hang it up.

JILL. I'm going to use it again. *(Starts off and up the stairs.)*

HARRIET. *(commandingly)* I don't want you to go back to the hospital; I want you to stay here.

JILL. You what?

HARRIET. You heard me.

JILL. You're giving me orders now?

HARRIET. I'm the oldest.

JILL. *(Returns to the room.)* I'll do as I please.

HARRIET. Can we try and get along through this? It would make things easier.

JILL. Why do I want to blame you?

HARRIET. *(pause)* Blame me for what?

JILL. All the ... death.

HARRIET. *(taken aback)* *I* didn't poison my father, *I* didn't shoot my mother...

JILL. You don't care.

HARRIET. They dug their own graves.

JILL. I loved them.

HARRIET. And they loved you.

JILL. *(pause)* Harriet, they—

HARRIET. Oh, go take your shower.

JILL. *(long pause)* When are you going back to New York?

HARRIET. I'll take a leave of absence ... until things are straightened out here. I could come back on weekends until — I hadn't really thought about it.

JILL. I have. I won't be going to the Cape now to wait on table.

HARRIET. *(almost simultaneously)* "...wait on table." Aren't you glad.

JILL. I'm staying here. I'll take care of Cammy at least through the summer.

HARRIET. You don't have to.

JILL. I'm going to.

HARRIET. We can hire a nurse or something after she gets out of the hospital...

JILL. I'll be here with her.

HARRIET. There are enough immediate problems—

JILL. It's settled. *(Starts off.)*

HARRIET. Then I'll have to stay, too.

JILL. *(returning)* Through the summer?

HARRIET. Yes.

JILL. Why?

HARRIET. Why do you think, dummy?

JILL. Don't call me that.

HARRIET. Cammy will need so much attention.

JILL. *(pause)* Oh, Harriet...

HARRIET. You're not so dumb after all. We're not so different.

JILL. Yes, we are.

HARRIET. *(firmly)* You think you're going to get away with something, sister dear, but you're not.

JILL. *(pause)* Well, you'd better keep your eye on me.

HARRIET. You think you'll have the summer to convince Cammy to cut me out of her will. Over my dead body.

JILL. You said it.

CAMMY. *(from offstage)* Jill? Harriet?

HARRIET. Cammy?

(JILL speaks as CAMMY appears.)

JILL. What are you doing back here?

CAMMY. Don't be upset. I told Dr. Potter it was more important for the three of us to be together tonight. I *told* him to let me come home ... well, he drove me here. Don't look so upset. He'll be by in the morning ... to take me back to the hospital ... for tests. I promise not to die in my sleep. *(pause)* That's not funny, is it?

HARRIET. Sit down, Cammy.

CAMMY. Yes *(Begins to move slowly, HARRIET attempts to assist her.)* I'm fine, Harriet. I am not an invalid yet ... just a little ... off my pins. *(Sits.)* I did get *some* sleep. *(pause)* I hope I recover from all this.

JILL. *(sitting beside her)* I'll be here with you.

CAMMY. Oh, Jill ... oh, good. *(pause)* I feel better already.

HARRIET. And I'll be here through the summer.

CAMMY. You will?

HARRIET. *(sitting on other side of her)* Yes.

CAMMY. What about your job?

HARRIET. I can take a leave of absence.

JILL. I can manage things here.

HARRIET. We'll discuss it later, Jill.

CAMMY. Oh, I am so pleased. *(Reaches out a hand to each of them. They each take a hand.)* Well, we're all that's left now. We three. *(pause)* We need each other ... to get through this. *(pause)* How grateful I am to have both of you now. *(Sighs, and drops her hands into her lap.)* Would you make me a cup of tea?

JILL. *(rising)* Of course. HARRIET. *(rising)* Yes.

HARRIET. Do you want something to eat?

JILL. I'll get it.

CAMMY. Just tea, dear. *(looking at HARRIET.)* And Jill, would you get me my slippers from my room?

HARRIET. I'm Harriet.

CAMMY. Oh. Yes.

HARRIET. I'll get them.

CAMMY. *(as both start off)* Jill. Harriet. *(pause)* I'm lucky to have ... such devoted granddaughters. *(HARRIET Exits upstage right into CAMMY'S room, JILL Exits upstage left. CAMMY rises, and moves toward the puzzle table.)* And I won't have to change my will again. *(Hesitates, pause.)* Unless...

(Lights fade.)

THE END

FURNITURE PLOT

Stage Right: (against wall)
- Side table
- Practical chair

Downstage Right: (against wall)
- Easy chair

Center Stage:
- Sofa with three small pillows
- Coffee table
- Side table (left of sofa)
- Side table (right of sofa)
- 2 lamps (on side tables)

Downstage Right Center:
- Practical chair
- Card table
- Rug

Downstage Left Center:
- Chair (matching sofa)
- Rug

Stage Left: (against wall)
- Secretary
- Lamp (on secretary)
- Practical chair
- Wastebasket

Down Left:
Chair

Upstage, Hallway by Stairs:
Side table
Lamp (on side table)

Upstage, Center Wall:
Bookshelves (books, knicknacks, etc.)

PROPERTY PLOT

PRESET — Off L. :

Distressed African violet w/card (Jill)
Wine glass (Jill)
Martini glass (Jill)
Scotch glass (Brad)
2 small tumblers (Brad)
Bottle of brandy (Brad)
Bowl w/ice cream & cake & spoon (Harriet)

PRESET — Off R. :

Towel (Jill)
.45 pistol w/tote bag (Cammy)

ACT I

PRESET:

Sofa:

Three pillows

Coffee table:

3 magazines
Dish of peanuts
Martini glass (Peg)

Table L. of sofa:

Wine glass (Harriet)

Side table: (against L. wall)

6 African violets w/cards

Secretary: (against R. wall)
2 floral bouquets w/cards

Card table:
Jigsaw puzzle (Mark Twain) w/box

Sofa:
Afghan (on back of sofa)

Scene 1 to Scene 2:
Strike dish of peanuts
Strike Cammy's martini glass on card table

ACT II

PRESET — Off L. :
Coffee mug, muffin, orange juice glass on tray (Jill)
Overnight bag (Harriet)
Purse (Harriet)
Bonzai tree (Harriet)
Sun glasses (Harriet)

PRESET — Off R. :
Sunglasses (Jill)
Garden gloves (Peg)
Bag of candy kisses (Cammy)

ACT III

PRESET — Off L. :
Coffee mug (Harriet)

PRESET — On Coffee Table:
Bag of candy kisses

SOUND CUES

ACT I
Phone ring

ACT II
Gunshot